# PIZZAS AND PANCAKES

An exciting range of recipes and useful tips – to break the
sandwich syndrome and provide varied and wholesome meals
in an economic way.

# PIZZAS AND PANCAKES

*by*

## JANET HUNT

*Illustrated by Clive Birch*

THORSONS PUBLISHERS LIMITED
Wellingborough, Northamptonshire

First published May 1982
Second Impression October 1982

British Library Cataloguing in Publication Data

Hunt, Janet
    Pizzas and pancakes.
    1. Vegetarian cookery
    2. Pancakes, waffles, etc.   3. Pizza
    I. Title
    641.5'636     TX837

    ISBN 0-7225-0723-2

Typeset by Glebe Graphics, Wilby, Northamptonshire.
Printed and bound in Great Britain by
Richard Clay (The Chaucer Press) Ltd.,
Bungay, Suffolk.

# CONTENTS

|                              | Page |
|------------------------------|------|
| Pizzas to Please             | 9    |
| Basic Dough Recipes          | 13   |
| Topping Ideas                | 19   |
| Making Pancakes              | 63   |
| Pancake Batters              | 67   |
| Savoury Fillings             | 73   |
| Pancakes with a Difference   | 101  |
| Sweet-tooth Crêpes           | 111  |
| *Index*                      | 127  |

Wholefoods, quite simply, are foods in their natural state – nothing added, nothing taken away. In this age of mass-production foods, wholefoods are not always easy to obtain. But as nutritionalists and doctors become increasingly convinced, of their value in building and maintaining health, so their availability is fast improving.

Include as many natural, unadulterated foods as you can in your day to day eating pattern, and discover not just exciting new tastes and a fresh approach to mealtimes, but better health too.

# PIZZAS TO PLEASE

It was not so long ago that if you wanted to eat pizza you had to go to Italy. Limited food supplies, particularly in the poverty-stricken South, had to be stretched to feed large families, and the pizza was one of the dishes that resulted from this need. A tasty combination of dough base (often stale bread!) and vegetable topping, with a tiny amount of cheese, fish or meat, it offered carbohydrate and protein and was as filling as it was inexpensive.

In recent years, however, pizza has become one of the world's most popular fast-foods. You can now enjoy it in elegant restaurants, corner cafés and canteens. Pubs serve it with a pint. Supermarkets offer do-it-yourself kits as well as the frozen variety. And take-away pizza parlours are everywhere. Pizzas can be a meal or a snack; can be enjoyed hot or cold; eaten with knife and fork, or served in slices to be held in the hand and munched like a sandwich. And those who haven't eaten it one way or another are rare - it really does seem to appeal to everyone.

The fact that pizzas are so readily available is probably one of the reasons so few people make their own. Another one may be that the traditional dough is made from yeast, and so takes a little more effort and time than many other home-made dishes. In fact, pizzas can be made without too much trouble. And for the 'wholefooder' they offer a perfect solution to the family with the big appetite and the small budget, as well as being a sneaky but highly successful way to get children who prefer junk foods to eat healthily – and enjoy it. When eating pizza out, the variety of toppings is usually rather limited, and the resulting dish nowhere near as nutritious as it could be, (unless, of course, you are eating at a wholefood restaurant). Make your pizza at home and you can make it a real 'health' food.

Substitute a crunchy, wholemeal crust for the pasty, tasteless dough made with refined white flour, and you've already added protein, fibre and vitamins. There are a variety of ways you can make this crust, both with and without yeast. It is a good idea, if the topping is going to be rather liquid, to bake the base in the oven for ten minutes first, so that it does not absorb too much liquid. If, however, you are not too fussed about such details, forget it – there are people who prefer their pizzas this way! You can also bake the dough until completely cooked, then add the topping and heat through briefly in the oven or under the grill – ideal if the topping ingredients do not need cooking (or if you simply prefer to get the maximum goodness from them, and eat them virtually raw). Always grease your baking sheet lightly before putting the dough onto it; you can also brush a light film of oil over the pizza base before adding the topping, and a little more oil over the actual topping ingredients (delicate vegetables such as mushrooms have a tendency to dry out if not protected this way).

How you shape your pizza is also up to you. Traditionally, pizzas are round and you can make one per person, or a large version to be served in slices. You can also make your dough oblong in shape and cook it in a Swiss roll tin, then cut into slices.

For even quicker pizzas, use wholemeal bread, Greek pitta bread, crispbreads or crackers as your base – add tomatoes, cheese, herbs, etc. and simply pop under the grill for a few minutes.

Deep-dish pizzas are not made on a baking sheet, but in a flan dish. The proportion of ingredients is therefore changed so that you have less dough and more filling, and they are served in wedges (although again, you could make very small individual ones and serve one to each person).

The traditional southern Italian pizza contained toma-toes and cheese, usually mozarella and/or Parmesan. In other parts of Italy the ingredients changed according to what was available locally, but these basics still tended to be used even if in lesser amounts. They also occur in many of the recipes in this book, but you can vary them as you (and your family) like. Quantities, too, can be adapted to fit in with what you have available – unlike many recipes, pizzas really cannot go wrong. If you use wholesome fresh ingredients, and don't overcook them, the results are bound to be tasty.

When you have learned to be adventurous with your pizza making, try experimenting with ideas of your own. Most vegetables, steamed or *sautéed*, make a moist contrast to the crisp dough. Other cheeses will change the character completely – try Danish blue, Gruyère, ricotta. Or forget about cheese altogether and sprinkle your pizza with cooked beans, lightly fried breadcrumbs, poached or scrambled eggs or bean sprouts. Many left-overs can be mashed, flavoured with herbs, and put under the grill for a few minutes to make an unusual topping for pizza. Soya meat in a thick sauce, or mixed with other ingredients, adds lots of protein as well as flavour. Tofu bean curd can be chopped, lightly fried, mixed with vegetables and sesame seeds, and spread over the dough. Nuts, seeds, herbs, spices – each will add something different and unique. The variations are restricted only by the obvious stipulation that you do not top your pizza with anything too liquid (it will drain away) or too chunky (it will slide off!). And watch the cooking temperature – the dough needs a hot oven to cook properly, so if this is likely to ruin the topping, add it just before the dough is cooked, or cook it separately and pile on just before serving.

Cold pizzas can be quite as appetizing as hot ones. Use any left-overs as a party nibble, T.V. snack or instead of biscuits with coffee. A carefully wrapped slice will help brighten a lunch box (and break the sandwich syndrome!). Take cold pizza on a picnic or a ramble; serve it to unexpected guests on a salad or with soup. You can even heat it up again – add a little extra grated cheese or tomato *purée* and put it under the grill. And you can, of course, freeze any extra pizzas so that they are ready and waiting for the next time you fancy one.

If you haven't tried sweet pizzas, now is your chance. Like a crisp, biscuit-type flan base, the dough lends itself well to such combinations as fruit, jams and honey, nuts, etc., and it really isn't necessary to sweeten it (though you can, of course, if you prefer). Stick to the crisper kind of dough as pizzas served this way should be light and tasty rather than heavy and filling. Make them into small individual circles, or cook them in a Swiss roll tin and slice them before dishing up. The recipes here can be eaten hot or cold, as they are or with yogurt, cream or nut cream. Quantities are half of those suggested for savoury pizzas on the assumption that they will be a delicious 'extra' rather than the main part of the meal; you can always, of course, double the quantities (any left-overs, as with savouries, will be more than edible when cold).

*All recipes are for 4 people.*

# BASIC DOUGH RECIPES

## COOKED-IN-THE-PAN PIZZA

6oz (175g) plain wholemeal flour
1 good teaspoonful baking powder
Water to mix
Sea salt to taste
Vegetable oil for cooking

1. Mix together the flour, baking powder and salt in a bowl.

2. Add water gradually, kneading to make a dough.

3. Continue kneading until dough is smooth and soft, then divide into two, and roll out into thin rounds.

4. Pour a little oil into a heavy pan and heat until hot but not smoking, then turn down heat and cook pizza slowly for two minutes.

5. Turn the pizza, add topping, and continue cooking for a few minutes more, by which time the underside should be brown, and the topping hot right through.

*Note:* Makes 2 medium-sized or 3 small pizzas.

# PIZZA SICILIAN
## (fat and filling)

¼pt (150ml) warm water
8 oz (225g) plain wholemeal flour
½ tablespoonful dried yeast
1 tablespoonful vegetable oil
½ teaspoonful demerara raw cane sugar

1. Pour the water into a bowl and sprinkle on the yeast. Stir in the sugar, and set aside for 5 to 10 minutes, or until mixture is frothy.

2. Add the oil, then stir the liquid into the sifted flour.

3. Turn onto a floured board and use hands to knead the dough thoroughly until pliable and smooth.

4. Put dough in a greased bowl, cover with a damp cloth, and leave in a warm, draught-free spot until well risen. (Alternatively, you could lightly oil the surface of the dough and put it in a polythene bag, securing the end firmly.)

5. Knead briefly again, then divide dough into four and shape into circles: place on lightly greased baking sheets and return to a warm spot for 15-30 minutes more.

6. Bake blind at 400°F/205°C (Gas Mark 6) for 5 minutes or so to firm up the crust before adding the topping –this helps prevent it becoming soggy.

7. Add topping of your choice and cook 10-15 minutes more.

8. If the topping does not need to be cooked, but just heated through, you can bake the pizza dough for approximately 20 minutes, then add the topping ingredients immediately and put the pizza under the grill for a few minutes more.

*Note:* Makes 2 medium-sized or 4 small pizzas.

# PIZZA NEAPOLITAN
## (thin and crisp)

¼ pt (150 ml) warm water
8 oz (225 g) plain wholemeal flour
½ teaspoonful dried yeast
1 tablespoonful vegetable oil

1.  Sprinkle the yeast onto the warm water, stir, and set aside until the mixture bubbles.

2.  Stir in the oil, then gradually add the liquid to the sifted flour.

3.  When this becomes difficult, turn the dough onto a floured board and knead for 5-10 minutes to make a soft, elastic dough.

4.  Divide mixture into four, and roll out immediately to make four thin circles.

5.  Place on lightly greased baking sheets and pre-bake for 5 minutes at 400°F/205°C (Gas Mark 6).

6.  Arrange the topping on the crisp pizza bases and cook for 10-15 minutes more.

7.  If the topping does not need to be cooked, but just heated through, you can bake the pizza dough for approximately 20 minutes, then add the topping ingredients and put the pizza under the grill for a few minutes more.

*Note:* Makes 2 medium-sized or 4 small pizzas.

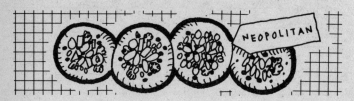

# SCONE DOUGH PIZZA

8 oz (225 g) self-raising wholemeal flour
2 oz (50 g) polyunsaturated margarine
Approx. ¼ pt (150 ml) milk
Pinch of sea salt

1. Sieve together the flour and salt.

2. Rub the margarine into the dry ingredients to make a crumb-like mixture.

3. Pour in enough milk to bind the mixture into a soft, manageable dough.

4. Turn onto a floured board and knead lightly.

5. Divide the dough into two and shape into thin rounds.

6. Arrange topping attractively, and bake pizzas at 400°F/205°C (Gas Mark 6) for 20-30 minutes, or until cooked.

*Note:* Makes 2 medium-sized or 4 small pizzas.

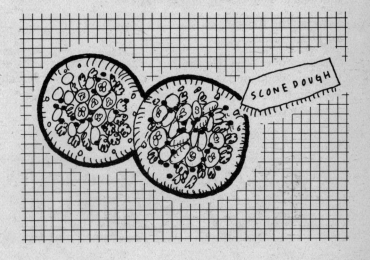

# PROTEIN-RICH PIZZA DOUGH

6 oz (175g) plain wholemeal flour
2 oz (50g) soya flour
1 tablespoonful dried yeast
¼ pt (150ml) warm water
1 tablespoonful vegetable oil
½ teaspoonful honey
Pinch of sea salt

1. Pour the water into a bowl, add the yeast and honey, and stir until both have dissolved.

2. Add the oil.

3. Sift together the flours and salt, and gradually add to the liquid, mixing well.

4. Turn dough onto a floured board and knead until supple.

5. Put in a greased bowl, cover, and leave in a warm place for 1 to 2 hours, or until doubled in size.

6. Knead again, then divide into four and shape into circles.

7. Roll out to about ⅛ in. thick and place on baking sheets.

8. Add topping and bake at 425°F/220°C (Gas Mark 7) for 15-20 minutes.

*Note:* Makes 2 medium-sized or 4 small pizzas.

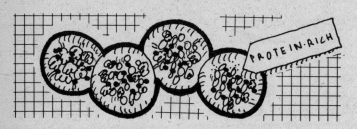

# TOPPING IDEAS

## PIZZA WITH ADUKI BEANS

Dough for 2 large or 4 small pizzas
8 oz (225g) aduki beans
1 teaspoonful thyme
1 teaspoonful ground coriander
Pinch of nutmeg
Vegetable oil or polyunsaturated margarine – optional
2 large tomatoes
12 green olives
Seasoning to taste

1. Soak beans overnight, then cook in plenty of water until soft.

2. Make up the pizza bases according to instructions.

3. Drain the beans and mash, or put into a blender, to make a smooth thick *purée*.

4. Stir in the spices and seasoning and, if the mixture seems too dry, just a little oil or margarine.

5. Smooth onto prepared pizza bases and top with slices of tomato and halved, stoned olives.

6. Bake at 400°F/205°C (Gas Mark 6) for approximately 20 minutes, or until base is crisp.

# CREAMY MUSHROOM PIZZA

Dough for 2 large or 4 small pizzas
1 large onion
½ clove garlic
12 oz (350g) firm mushrooms
1 tablespoonful vegetable oil
1 oz (25g) plain wholemeal flour
½ pt (275 ml) creamy milk, milk with 1 tablespoonful
   skimmed milk powder added, or soya milk
1-2 teaspoonsful dill
Chives to garnish
Seasoning to taste

1. Prepare the pizza bases; bake blind for 15 minutes.

2. Clean and slice the mushrooms; steam briefly, then drain well.

3. Chop the onion finely, then *sauté* for a minute or two with the crushed garlic in the vegetable oil.

4. Add the flour and cook until it begins to colour.

5. Remove from heat; pour in the milk; return to cooker and bring to boil, stirring continually.

6. Add mushrooms, herbs and seasoning; simmer until sauce thickens.

7. Pour onto pizza bases and spread evenly; (if sauce is too thick, add more liquid; if too runny, thicken with a little fine oatmeal).

8. Sprinkle with chopped chives and cook until heated through.

# PIZZA 'SCAPRICCIATELLO'

Dough for 2 large or 4 small pizzas
8 oz (225g) ripe tomatoes
4 oz (100g) mozzarella cheese
2 oz (50g) ham-flavoured soya 'meat chunks'
1 medium red pepper
4 oz (100g) mushrooms
1 tablespoonful vegetable oil
20 green olives
1 small tin artichokes or fresh equivalent
4 oz (100g) grated Parmesan cheese
1-2 teaspoonsful oregano
Seasoning to taste

1.  Prepare pizza bases, bake blind for 10 minutes, and set aside.

2.  Clean, slice and lightly fry the mushrooms. Drain on a paper towel.

3.  Hydrate the soya meat, according to pack instructions.

4.  Distribute the soya meat, sliced artichokes and mushrooms across the pizza bases.

5.  Peel and mash the tomatoes; spread them over the other ingredients and sprinkle with oregano. Season well.

6.  Slice the mozzarella thinly and lay on top of pizzas, then arrange olives and strips of pepper over cheese. Sprinkle with Parmesan.

7.  Bake for 10 minutes more until mozzarella melts, and dough is completely cooked.

# POTATO PIZZA

Dough for 2 large or 4 small pizzas
8 small potatoes, preferably new
1 lb (450g) ripe tomatoes
2 large onions
1 tablespoonful vegetable oil
1 tablespoonful basil or oregano
1 clove crushed garlic
Grated Parmesan cheese
10 olives
Parsley to garnish
Seasoning to taste

1.  Make up the pizza bases and set aside.

2.  Steam the potatoes until just tender, cool slightly, then slice as thin as possible and arrange attractively on pizza dough.

3.  Heat the vegetable oil and lightly *sauté* the sliced onion and garlic for 3 minutes.

4.  Wash and chop the tomatoes and add to the onion with herbs and seasoning; cook until mixture is thick, and most of the liquid has dried up.

5.  Pour sauce over potatoes, spreading it evenly. Sprinkle with cheese, decorate with halved, stoned olives and bake at 400°F/205°C (Gas Mark 6) for 20-25 minutes.

6.  Garnish with fresh, chopped parsley.

# FENNEL PIZZA

Dough for 2 large or 4 small pizzas
1½lb (675g) fennel bulbs of similar size
1 medium onion
½ clove garlic
4oz (100g) polyunsaturated margarine
2 tablespoonsful vegetable oil
1-2 teaspoonsful basil
4oz grated Parmesan cheese
3 large ripe tomatoes
Parsley to garnish
Seasoning to taste

1.  Prepare the pizza dough and bake blind for 10 minutes.

2.  Remove the outer leaves and stems from the fennel bulbs, wash, cut into quarters, and dry well.

3.  In a saucepan melt 2oz (50g) margarine with the oil, then add the fennel and cook gently for a few minutes.

4.  Add a spoonful or two of water, cover pan, and simmer for 20 minutes, or until tender.

5.  In another pan, heat 2oz (50g) margarine, add the sliced onion and crushed garlic, and cook briefly.

6.  Chop or mash the peeled tomatoes and add to the onion, with the basil and seasoning. Cook until a sauce-like mixture forms.

7.  Arrange the drained fennel on the pizza bases, and spread with the tomato sauce; top with grated Parmesan and heat for 10 minutes more.

8.  Serve garnished with chopped parsley.

# CABBAGE AND NUT PIZZA

Dough for 2 large or 4 small pizzas
½ medium white cabbage
4 oz (100g) cream or curd cheese
2 oz (50g) almonds
1 teaspoonful marjoram
1 teaspoonful oregano
Seasoning to taste

1. Prepare pizza bases, bake blind for 15 minutes, and set aside.

2. Shred the cabbage very fine and steam until just tender, then drain.

3. Stir the cheese into the cabbage until it melts, then add seasoning and herbs.

4. Spoon mixture onto pizzas and spread evenly.

5. Chop nuts coarsely and scatter over top.

6. Heat through for 5-10 minutes.